Ordering Our Steps

Committing Life and Sport to Christ

Leo R. Sayles

Edited by Faith Sayles

ISBN-13: 978-0-692-12420-8

PRAISE FOR COACH SAYLES

"In my years as the editor of *Sharing the Victory* magazine (now *FCA Magazine*), I was always looking for quality content that we could share through our ministry's daily Impact Play devotion. Leo Sayles was one of our finest contributors. As a coach himself, he truly understood the competitive mindset and how to turn athletic situations into spiritual and life lessons. Whenever I saw that Leo had sent a new devotion, I knew it would be one worth sharing immediately. I'm thankful for his gift of writing that corresponds with his gift of coaching and hope that each devotion in this book brings new insight and blessing to the lives of the readers."

Jill Lee, Communications Manager, Premier Sports Management; formerly Editor, FCA Magazine, FCA's Impact daily email devotion

"It is because my good friend Leo Sayles is a committed follower of Christ and an outstanding head coach that he can write such an inspiring devotional. This book demonstrates his wonderful gift of sharing observations from the world of sports while at the same time helping us see practical truths from God's Word. Coach Sayles' insights will challenge you 'to press on toward the goal to win the prize for which God has called [us] heavenward in Christ Jesus' (Philippians 3:14)."

Tracy C. Jessup, Gardner-Webb University Vice President for Christian Life and Service, Senior Minister to the University

"As one of Leo's former athletes and as a current coach I can attest to the importance of being at the top of your game not only physically, but mentally and spiritually as well. Anyone with the heart of an athlete will find Leo speaking directly into your life and experience to sharpen you for the challenges that lie ahead. This is a resource that should be in the hands of every coach and athlete!"
Gerad Hall, Stewardship Representative, Moody Global Ministries

CONTENTS

	Acknowledgments	i
	Foreword	iii
	Introduction	v
1	How's Your Foundation	1
2	Longing for More	4
3	Chosen for the Team	7
4	God Qualifies the Called	10
5	Dream Big	14
6	God's Game Plan	17
7	New Opportunities, New Realities	21
8	Win-Win Situation	25
9	Mastering the Ordinary	28
10	Forward Progress	31
11	Desire	34
12	Spreading the Salt	37
13	It's All About Heart	40
14	Order My Steps: The Right Direction	43
15	Stick to the Plan	46

16	Defining Moments	49
17	Whatever You Do, Do Heartily	53
18	Home Crowd: Cloud of Witnesses	57
19	Pride is a Team-Killer	60
20	An Expensive Mistake	63
21	Getting Back on the Right Path	67
22	Words of Grace	71
23	Two are Better Than One	74
24	Hope: Eager Expectation	77
25	Christian Hope	80
26	Diligence	83
27	Heart of a Champion	86
28	Stand Firm	89
29	Dedication	92
30	He Must Increase	95
31	Fought the Good Fight	98
	Sources	101
	About the Editor and Graphic Designer	105

ACKNOWLEDGMENTS

I thank God for blessing me with the gift to connect with people through written and oral communication. It is both humbling and awesome to know He granted me the opportunity to share His truths to impact athletes and coaches through the realm of sports.

Coaches Robert Turner and Roland Ortmayer, for inspiring me to pursue coaching through their influence as coaches during critical periods of my life

Jill Lee, former editor of FCA IMPACT devotions, for supporting and encouraging me to continue writing

Pastors Scott Boerckel and David Saylor, for mentoring me in ministry and proving valuable sources of wisdom and wit through their sermons and lessons during my years serving under their leadership

Dr. Sanford Zensen for providing my first position as a college coach and mentoring our staff in Christian leadership.

Matt Bollant, Deane Webb, Mike Simpson, Rick Reeves, Rusty Stroupe, Tee Burton, and many others in the coaching profession, for modeling what it means to be a Christian Coach and providing tips, advice, and perspective.

My wife, Tanya, for consistently supporting my ministry efforts and serving as a sounding board and advisor for many sermons and devotions throughout the years

My brother, Kevin Sayles, for first publishing his own book and encouraging me for years to publish

Many other family, friends, and students for encouraging me to continue writing and speaking to the heart through my sport-related devotions.

Special thanks to my friend and former co-worker, Jamy Bechler (@JamyBechler), for his encouragement and guidance throughout the editing and publishing process.

Finally, my daughter, Faith Sayles, for having the courage and drive to take on the challenge of editing her father's work. Seeing your daughter take something you have done for years and elevate it to a higher level is very special. I am humbled and proud to see how much further she has taken the gift of writing and am thrilled at her service in this endeavor…even though it means I am at the beck and call of my daughter to complete this project!

Soli Deo Gloria

FOREWORD

I love sports. Like many of you, I grew up watching and playing a variety of sports - volleyball, soccer, basketball, ultimate frisbee, tennis, track, swimming...you name it and I probably tried to either play or learn about the sport. I have my father to thank for this love of sports.

In my 22 years, my father has always been coaching something. When I was born, he was teaching and coaching high school boys and girls track and volleyball at the local high school (while volunteering in ministry positions at our church) but transitioned into a full-time pastor position while continuing to coach on the side by the time I was 3. I was 5 when we moved to the Midwest where he had accepted a youth pastor position and coached high school track and soccer. When I was 8, he took the full-time women's volleyball coaching position at Bryan College in Tennessee.

For the next 7 ½ years, I watched my father pour into the lives of all kinds of athletes, not just his volleyball girls. Due to homeschooling, we (my mother, my 4 siblings, and I) had the freedom to follow my father all over the United States as we cheered for his team. We watched the ups and downs of the volleyball program. We accompanied my father to the college's other athletic events as we supported the other teams. Everyone on campus knew whose children we were.

Looking back on those years, I appreciate how my father set aside time to coach our YMCA sports teams and attend our sporting events. In his camp-filled summers, he would take one or two of us with him for the camps, so we could spend time with him. His job is a time-consuming one, but he always made time for us - tickle fights, cooking together, setting off fireworks, playing games. We had a lot of fun.

As I grew older, I realized that my father was always coaching or teaching. Sometimes, we children found it annoying. We'd be in the middle of a rousing game of Risk, each of us trying to take over the world, and he would start coaching the pouting child on how to best take over the world. But that just emphasizes to me how strongly coaching is ingrained in him.

In this book, we have collected 31 sports inspired devotions that my father wrote over the past 12 years. These devotions expound on specific qualities, virtues, and achievements that are often developed in athletes such as devotion, desire, and teamwork. We pray that you will find some wisdom and values to share with your fellow athletes and coaches.

Faith Sayles, editor
faithsayles.org

INTRODUCTION

This devotion book is dedicated to the mentors who have helped shape my adult life. On paper, my adult life seems to follow three "career" tracks; a music educator, a pastor, and an athletic coach. A scarlet thread runs through my story, a common denominator that transcended my different "careers;" my involvement with sports. Some very special coach mentors, especially one affectionately known as "Ort," stoked my passion for sports.

I was led to a relationship with Christ at age 11 by a relative. Without a connection to a church, I floundered through my teen years. By age 16, my parents had divorced, and I went through a rebellious stage, which reached its zenith when I seriously injured my knee after taking a dare from a friend. During my recovery God led me to my first coaching experience (you'll learn more in one of my devotions). As I recommitted my life to Christ, I realized that God was turning my poor choices into a positive experience that would shape my adult life and ministry. My high school track coach and high school choir director were tremendous role models who kept me in line enough to get me on my feet again.

My college years were tumultuous, mixed with great moments, family struggles, tragedy, heartache, and triumphs. I bounced around colleges before I finally settled at the University of La Verne, a small Division III university back in my hometown of La Verne, CA. There, I got back on my feet, majored in vocal music, and ran track (there was a very brief experiment with football as well). Once again, I was blessed with tremendous role models. My college choir director (who became my father-in-law) supported my athletic endeavors and taught me many valuable teaching lessons that still guide me today. My high school track coach brought me on staff and mentored me for three years as a coach. However, Coach Ortmayer was the adult who had the most influence in my life and work as a coach. Roland Ortmayer (1917 – 2008) was the legendary NAIA Hall of Fame football coach who impacted lives for 6 decades at the University of La Verne. ULV's coach for 43 years, he was known as the man who didn't use a playbook, lined the fields himself, and washed each uniform himself every Friday before our big game that weekend.

But his greatest gift was loving the young men who called him 'Coach.' His distinctive style, personality, and influence shaped the lives of hundreds of young men and women who came through the doors and onto the football field and track at La Verne. His legendary status at ULV was picked up by Sports Illustrated in 1989, when Douglas Looney ran an article entitled, "A Most Unusual Man." That article led to a special report by ABC World News Tonight and legendary fame across the country.

I was privileged to call him my coach on the track and on the field for a short period of time. As a young athlete, I was always told I was too small to compete in football. I loved the game, watched my older brother play into high school, and always dreamed of taking the field. In college, I met Ort and ran track under him for two seasons…but my senior year, I was encouraged to walk on with the football team because the team needed more speed in their receiving core. I would love to say that I had a tremendous experience and became a critical component of the team, but that would be a lie. I walked onto the field in 1988 as a 5'6" 145-pound receiver, and I found the game was much tougher to play on the field then in the sandlot. I did not have "soft" enough hands to catch the ball well. My speed was fine, but I struggled learning routes, and I learned that 'crack-blocking' does a world of hurt to a little receiver's body. But Ort and his staff gave me the chance, and my brother and friends rallied around me as I tried. I remember one specific practice, when my 72-yr old coach picked up a ball, had me run patterns on the side of the field, and threw passes to me while the rest of the team continued to practice. His personal care to help me be my best has always guided me.

Even though he extended grace, patience, and love to me on the field, there were two experiences off the field that forever shaped my future. Each season, Coach Ort and his wife, Corny, would have a couple of players over for dinner a few nights out of the week. My brother and I went together for dinner one night, and I learned why this gentle coach took such a personal interest in each of his players. After dinner while talking over a bowl of ice-cream, Ort shared about being the consummate coach years before: spending many long hours watching video, scouting, and devising plays for his teams.

On one occasion, as he was preparing for a baseball field preparation session, his son David, who wanted to go fishing, was with him. He felt that he could not and proceeded out to the field assuming his son would soon follow. Later that day, he received a devastating call. His son had drowned in a fishing accident. Overcome with grief, this man found solace in his faith, and made a vow to God that he would never again be consumed by conventional success but, instead, would focus his energies investing his life into others the way he wished he could for his lost son. That night, I left his home profoundly moved, and found I loved and respected this man because of his love for me. I desired to learn from his lesson, to love my children while at the same time impacting my athletes through my personal investment in their lives.

Ort showed me his caring nature again that next spring during my final year of track. There were only a handful of runners on the team, so Ort would sometimes send us to track meets on our own. On one Friday, we received confusing information about an invitational in which I was to run. That morning, I was told the meet started that afternoon. I called Coach Ort, who promptly cancelled his classes, excused me from class, and offered to drive me to the university where the meet was to be held. We drove the 90-minute trip together, and talked about God, our faith, and life. When we arrived at the track, not a soul was to be found. The meet was to be on Saturday. I felt so bad and apologized again and again to my coach…but he chuckled, smiled at me, and said, "It was well worth the time to have some quality minutes with you." I will always remember that drive and the deep impression he left on my life.

Coach Ort's football record floated around .500 over his career…but his win percentage in the lives he has impacted has to be near a thousand. I found success as a teacher, youth pastor and now as a college volleyball coach; as I peer into the eyes of every player who comes under my tutelage, I remember Ort's life-goal - to invest into the lives of the students who came across his path. I've hoped that I too could impact lives as he had mine.

Through my years of coaching, I see constant reminders of the Christian life in sports moments. I've used sports analogies throughout my years in ministry and started writing and speaking for FCA when I became a college coach. This book is a compilation of those devotions. My simple prayer is that these short devotions will uplift you and encourage you to order your steps in a life committed to the Lord.

Leo R. Sayles

1.

HOW'S YOUR FOUNDATION?

Therefore, everyone who hears these words of Mine and acts on them, may be compared to a wise man who built his house on the rock. And the rain fell, and the floods came, and the winds blew and slammed against that house; and yet it did not fall, for it had been founded on the rock. Everyone who hears these words of Mine and does not act on them, will be like a foolish man who built his house on the sand. The rain fell, and the floods came, and the winds blew and slammed against that house; and it fell—and great was its fall.
Matthew 7:24-27

In 2012, one of my sons learned a painful lesson about foundations.

A plyometrics box is meant for jumping on or off; it's a great tool that people can use with confidence. The box is like the foundation Christ seeks for each of us. Some people build their house on the sandy ground...but others start on the firm foundation. However, the enemy creeps in and slowly chips away at their foundation...until they are left with nothing but a ball.

Have you ever tried standing on a basketball? My (at the time) 13-year-old son did...and the results were not pretty.

Earlier in the week, my son had broken his shoulder, and still had his arm in a shoulder-stabilizing sling the night of this painful incident. For some reason that he still cannot explain, he decided to stand on the ball, with his one free hand holding onto a nearby stage for balance. As he did so,

1

his brother came into the hall...so what does my son do? He tried to wave hello to his brother, taking his free hand off the stage. You can imagine the result...my son knocked himself out when he fell face first onto the floor.

After throwing up for an hour, being strapped to a backboard for 3 hours, taking an ambulance ride to the hospital, enduring a cat scan, receiving 7 stitches, and suffering 24 hours of amnesia, we asked him what happened. His response was classic: "I was being stupid."
He learned a valuable lesson: You need a firm foundation on which to stand.

In May 2012, Tullian Tchividjian, the pastor at Coral Ridge Presbyterian Church (Fort Lauderdale, FL), shared a tweet that read, "We often rest our Christianity on the crumbling foundation of our imperfect devotion to Jesus rather than on his perfect devotion to us."[1]

We must ask ourselves, "How is my foundation?"

If we identify with the wise man, then our foundation is built on Christ and His commands. However, if we have built upon the foundation of self, allowing the world to water down God's truth, filter out God's voice, and blot out God's commands...we will find ourselves facing the plight of the foolish man. And when the storms of life come, and they *will* come, great will be our fall. Let's walk circumspectly, look inward, and make sure that we are building on the *firm foundation of Christ*.

Questions

1. What daily steps do you take in practice to strengthen foundational skills for your sport?
2. What steps can you take to strengthen your spiritual foundation?

Further Reading

Luke 6:46-49; 1 Corinthians 3:10-17

Notes

2.

LONGING FOR MORE

O God, You are my God; I shall seek You earnestly;
My soul thirsts for You, my flesh yearns for You,
In a dry and weary land where there is no water.
Thus, I have seen You in the sanctuary,
To see Your power and Your glory.
Psalm 63:1-2

There is a common bond that seems to separate good teams from great teams – hunger.

Good teams have the capability of winning at any time, but somehow lack what it takes to do it day-in and day-out. Great teams seem to always find a way – whether they play the perfect match, have to slug out a tough win, or find a way to come clawing back after trailing. They just seem to find a way to win. For many of them, it is because of a hunger for victory. Great teams crave winning. It is like the hunger for that food you love and cannot get enough of. Champions seem to savor the victory and, yet, still crave more.

In my years as a worship leader, part of my job was to teach people, through song and Scripture, to yearn for more in their relationship with Christ. However, some Christians perceive the concept of "hungering to win" in sport competition as wrong. I don't see any problem with wanting to win. In fact, I see it as a great opportunity to teach athletes how to have that same "hunger to win" in their relationship with Christ!

4

In today's passage, David expresses this hunger in a way that we can all understand. Just as great athletes have a hunger for victory, David's hunger for God was insatiable. In verses 3-5, he expresses the depth of satisfaction he receives from walking with the Lord and how it drives him to seek God more.

Paul expressed the same hunger for Christ in Philippians 3. It drove him to not be satisfied with anything this world could offer him.

Christ's touch on our lives should never cause us to sit back and stop pursuing Him. It should create a deeper hunger and thirst for the One who will wipe away every tear at the "Great Wedding Feast," the end of times. God gives us glimpses of our future with Him to keep us longing for more. Let's crave our wins on the court...and let's hunger for more of Christ each day!

Questions

1. How have coaches worked to create a competitive hunger in you as a player?
2. How do you sustain a vibrant hunger for Christ on a daily basis?

Further Reading
Philippians 3:7-16; Psalm 84:1-3

Notes

3.

CHOSEN FOR THE TEAM

*But we should always give thanks to God for you, brethren beloved by
the Lord, because God has chosen you from the beginning for salvation
through sanctification by the Spirit and faith in the truth.*
2 Thessalonians 2:13

Some years ago, while watching commentary regarding that
year's NFL draft, I was reminded of the special feeling
players feel when they are chosen for a team. Whether
being picked to be on a sandlot team, making the cut for
the varsity team, being recruited to a college team, or being
drafted to a professional organization, there is a wonderful
sense of acceptance and gratitude one feels when "making
the team."

I can remember as a freshman in high school walking up to
the basketball coach's door to see if my name was on his list
after tryouts. I can remember grinning happily and high-
fiving friends who made the team with me. I felt called,
chosen, set apart for a unique purpose; I was "part of the
team."

Paul, in his second letter to the Thessalonian church wrote,
"From the beginning God chose you to be saved". But we
were not just chosen to be saved. We were chosen to be
God's workmanship (Ephesians 2:10). Peter carries this
concept further in 1 Peter 2:9-10. In his epistle, he
proclaims that we are a chosen generation and a priesthood
to proclaim God to the world.

Just as each rookie is drafted with a purpose and a plan for his role in the organization, God has chosen us to be a part of *His* plan to unite souls with Him. We each have a unique role to play, based on the gifts, desires, and talents He placed in us before we knew Him. Just as a rookie's job is to learn his role and meet the requirements necessary to fulfill that role, we must individually take time to understand God's plan for us and fulfill our role in the church and community around us.

When Jesus spoke to the disciples in John 13-17, He stated that God's plan is simple yet profound:

      1) Abide in Him
      2) Love one another
      3) Keep His commands
      4) Go and make disciples.

We have been chosen for God's Master Plan. We have been consecrated for His service. Will you put on His jersey and fulfill His plan?

Questions

1. Have you experienced being chosen for a team or organization (a choir, dance ensemble, drama group, academic team)? If so, how did you feel when you found you "made the team?"

2. As a chosen child of God, what steps can you take daily to represent God's "team?"

Further Reading

Ephesians 2:8-10; 1 Peter 2:9-12

Notes

4.

GOD QUALIFIES THE CALLED

You did not choose Me, but I chose you and appointed you that you should go and bear fruit, and that your fruit should remain, that whatever you ask the Father in My name He may give you.
John 15:16

In the spring of 2004, I served as a youth pastor at a church in East Moline, IL. The ministry was progressing well, but I found a burning passion to work primarily with college students and athletes. It was the result of several years developing a college ministry, which culminated with a sport mission trip to the Dominican Republic.

Throughout my tenure at the church, I had a godly pastor who mentored me and gave me direction. As we discussed and prayed about my future in ministry, I chose to apply for several opportunities at Christian universities. I pursued ministry positions and coaching opportunities in volleyball and track. The application process progressed through the spring. Several ministry opportunities were offered, but I felt led to decline them. However, the pursuit of coaching positions was proving fruitless, and I was about to give up the process when I was contacted by Bryan College (Dayton, TN) to interview for their volleyball head coach position.

As I prepared for the interview, I knew that I did not necessarily meet the qualifications most universities sought; I had no college playing or coaching experience and was not currently coaching any high school team. I prepared to justify my work in ministry and was determined to show that I was indeed up to the task.

When I began the interview, the athletic director first told me his story. As a former senior pastor who also coached soccer at a local high school, Dr. Sanford Zensen felt God directing him to a more focused ministry, pouring into the lives of young men and guiding younger coaches in their careers. As the interview continued, I realized God was placing me under the tutelage of a person with the same passion and calling.

I may not have met the conventional qualifications for the position, but God was calling me...and this godly Athletic Director heard that call. I was granted the position in the late spring and launched a new phase of my ministry to young adults. I may not have been qualified, but God called!

Throughout scripture, God has qualified the called. A quote from an unknown source that has circulated in sermons and devotions reads:

Jacob was a liar, David had an affair, Noah got drunk, Jonah ran from God, Paul was a murderer, Gideon was insecure, Martha was a worrier, Sarah laughed at God's promises, Elijah was moody, Moses stuttered, Abraham was old... and Lazarus was dead. God doesn't call the qualified, He qualifies the CALLED![2]

We are all seeking God's Will for us, trying to be useful to Him. Perhaps the focus is wrong.

Jesus said he chose us – to abide in *Him,* to be in relationship with Him. In so doing, He empowers us to be useful, in the right place, at the right time.

In making us disciples, God does not build on any natural capacity of ours. He does not ask us to do things that are naturally easy for us. He only asks us to do to the things that we are perfectly fit to do through His grace.

Doing His work is less about me, and more about His supernatural ability to mold and make me fit for His perfect plan. If I will remain focused on my relationship with Him, then I can say, "here am I, send me!"

No matter where you are in your life with God, He is qualifying you for His service because you are *called*. He can help you overcome the hurdles in your life or the mistakes you have made, and even use them to help others. Just allow *Him* to use you.

Questions

1. As a player or coach, has there been a time when you were reluctant to take on a new challenge (try out for a team or position, seek a leadership role or new position)? If so, how did you overcome that reluctance?

2. What are you afraid to attempt in life because you do not feel qualified?

Further Reading

1 Samuel 16; John 6:1-13; 1 Corinthians 1:27-29;
2 Corinthians 12:9

Notes

5.

DREAM BIG

Joseph had a dream.
Genesis 37:5a

Have you ever been a part of a team that had a breakthrough year? In my own experience as both a player and a coach, those occasions have happened after much planning and training. "Miracle" seasons don't just "happen." Regardless of how hard a coaching staff plans or how much a team trains, if they don't dream big, they cannot hope to achieve something beyond themselves.

In Genesis 37, scripture tells us Joseph had a dream. He didn't just have one; he had two. When he shared the dreams with his brothers, they completely understood the meaning – that Joseph would be elevated above them. Verse 11 says the brothers envied him…but his father pondered the meaning of these dreams.

Scripture does not explicitly say the dream came from God, but the implication is there. In the ensuing trials he endured, Joseph must have treasured those dreams in his heart. They gave him hope when times looked hopeless and strength when his hope ran out. I am sure it also sustained him when he was in the depth of despair.

For championship teams, it is a foregone conclusion that they will dream big. They set goals that others may believe are impossible. They envision the rewards at the end of their dream, and that big vision carries them through the trials and tribulations that come with any competitive season.

Do we do the same in our own lives? Do we ever take inventory of our gifts, turn them over to God, and say, "use me to build your kingdom?"

We have a Heavenly Father who has hard-wired us with our gifts, talents, and desires to be His instruments. When we allow His Spirit to guide our lives, a power is unleashed in us that the gates of Hell cannot prevail against! We need to dream like Joseph, and pray like Jabez, "Oh, that you would bless me and enlarge my territory!" (1 Chronicles 4:10).

William Faulkner once said, "Always dream and shoot higher than you know you can do."[3]

Do you believe God has implanted an impossible dream within your heart? If so, be sure your dream is in line with scripture and stays within the boundaries of His will. Then prayerfully put together a plan of action to see that dream to fruition. For God, "who is able to do *far more abundantly* beyond all that we ask or think, according to the power that works within us" (Eph 3:20), will guide you on the path to see that dream become reality.

Questions

1. What steps have you taken to fulfill your "Big Dream" for your team?
2. If God has implanted a "Big Dream" in your heart, what steps are you taking to fulfill that dream?

Further Reading

Genesis 37-45 (the entire story of Joseph);
1 Chronicles 4:9-10

Notes

6.

GOD'S GAME PLAN

But we speak God's wisdom in a mystery, the hidden wisdom which God predestined before the ages to our glory; the wisdom which none of the rulers of this age has understood; for if they had understood it they would not have crucified the Lord of glory.
1 Corinthians 2:7-8

The 2010 NCAA basketball National Championship game between Duke and Butler was a classic, displaying two well-coached teams, two well-devised game plans, and a match that was not decided until *after* the final second ticked off the clock. Both coaches did their homework. They scouted their opponents and gleaned through every bit of information and video footage they could get their hands on. The players were well-informed, and everyone went forth with confidence that their plan would succeed.

The game, though not perfect, was filled with passion, desire, and determination. Both coaches could say afterward that sometimes their game-plan worked perfectly. An in-bounds play would result in a basket, or a defensive switch would work just as planned. But at other times, the ball just wouldn't bounce right. The defense got a hand on a pass, or someone simply missed an assignment.

Any experienced coach knows that this is the point where we go "off-book." Things get messy, and we learn to adjust and adapt, vary and modify. We keep the big picture in mind and alter the plan.

In Luke 24, the resurrected Jesus meets Cleopas and another disciple on the road to Emmaus. Scripture says that the men's eyes were restrained from recognizing Jesus. As Paul describes in today's scripture, they were unaware of God's hidden wisdom in Christ's crucifixion. However, Christ Himself would unravel the mystery for them.

He asked the disciples what they were talking about. They responded that they were discussing the crucifixion of the Messiah and the disappearance of His body. Jesus then presented the actual game plan—God's big picture and the role Jesus had to play in order to fulfill that plan. He clarifies for them all of the Scriptures concerning Himself. Later, as He breaks bread with them, their eyes were opened, and they realized who He is.

Just as a good coach proceeds into each match with a plan of action, God had a plan in place for the world. He also has a plan for you!

According to Genesis 1 and John 1, God existed before the beginning of time. In the heavenly realms, angels served Him; however, Isaiah 14 reveals that one of them (Satan) became prideful and broke from the plan by trying to place himself on equal footing with God. He was therefore cast out and, eventually, roamed the earth seeking to destroy and deceive God's children. Adam and Eve's run-in with him in Genesis 3 appeared to mess up God's plan.

God, however, had the final say. His plan was enacted and fulfilled through the life, death, and resurrection of Jesus Christ, and we, His people, have been rescued by Him.

The Book of Revelation reveals the outcome of this struggle between God and the enemy and gives us a glimpse into the completion of God's plan for us. As the Bible concludes in Revelation 22, Jesus wins and love conquers all!

The clock of time is still ticking. Unlike the college basketball championship, however, the outcome of the biggest "game" has already been decided. Jesus arose as proof that the game was won. Yes, we have an adversary who wants to keep us from living in that truth. He has a plan, as well, and is launching counter-attacks against us all the time.

We can live as if we are defeated, or we can claim the victory in Christ and rise up to live in victory with Him! In order to do so, we must know God's plan, so we can follow it as we compete and as we live.

Questions

1. Think back on times in which you or your coach drew up game plans for your matches. What did you do to fulfil the game plan?
2. In the spiritual life, the enemy is constantly seeking to thwart God's plan for our lives. What steps are you taking to stay within God's plan?

Further Reading

Jeremiah 29:11; Luke 24:13-35; Hebrews 10:12-14;
2 Peter 3:10-13

Notes

7.

NEW OPPORTUNITIES, NEW REALITIES

'For I know the plans that I have for you,' declares the LORD, 'plans for welfare and not for calamity to give you a future and a hope. Then you will call upon Me and come and pray to Me, and I will listen to you.'
Jeremiah 29:11-12

As the coach of a college fall sport, the winter months are a time of looking forward and planning ahead for me. We've finished reflecting on the past season, we've completed our exit interviews, and we've laid out the plans for spring training. Now our attention turns to filling open positions with recruits and envisioning what the team will look like. Veterans return from break ready to embrace the challenge of becoming smarter, better, and stronger. New recruits sign on with the hopes of becoming an important part of the program.

In every new season, we are presented with new opportunities, new challenges, new relationships, and new realities.

New Opportunities:
New opportunities abound for every new team. If a star player is graduating from the program, there is an opportunity for someone else to step up, for an incoming player to make an impact, or for a veteran to become the new go-to player. If the team failed to overcome a particular opponent in the previous season, there is a coming opportunity to win the "unwinnable" game. If there was a

particular goal that was unattainable, the team can set a higher standard.

New Challenges:
A new season means new questions to answer. We must determine what steps to take in order to reach our goal. We have to anticipate issues and potential struggles to build an effective plan that can withstand the possible storm.

New Relationships:
With a new season comes new personnel changes. We seek to recognize and train new team leaders. We must identify who will fill specific roles within the program, such as the caregiver, the stabilizer, and the winner. We must try to determine how the new players fit into the system. We hope to avoid friction and interpersonal conflict as the season launches.

New Realities:
One of the toughest questions to answer is preparing for the unanticipated. This can become a team energizer or the issue that drains the staff and team. How we prepare will determine how we handle these new realities.

Every team faces these issues, as does every individual. In sports, we build on the hope of a better season and a better year ahead. In life, we must do the same, depending on our Lord to see us through each new day.

In Genesis 8 and 9, Noah faced such challenges when God opened the door of the ark. He and his family had the opportunity to begin anew and to launch into a new world as they stepped off the ark onto dry land. However, there were new relationships that faced them. For the first time, God authorized that humans could eat meat; but with this new condition, God gave the animal kingdom fear and terror regarding humans. What a change in relationships! This new condition would drastically change the realities of daily life for Noah's family.

If you know the story, Noah and his family did not last long before sin started to show its ugly head. However, at the end of chapter 8, God made a promise that I believe helped the family continue forward. He said, from that time forth, the days, the seasons, and the years would not end. In other words, even if you should falter, the sun will rise again. That promise ties directly to Romans 8:28, "...all things work together for good, to those who love the Lord."

Any time we launch into a new year, we are presented with new opportunities and challenges. They will be accompanied by new relationships and realities which will change our horizons. Go forth and face those challenges with the knowledge that God is in control. He is going before you and He has your back. He will see you through!

Questions

1. How have you, your team, or staff approached new seasons?
2. As you face new opportunities (college, career, marriage, move, etc.), what steps will you take to anchor yourself in God's Word and plan?

Further Reading
Genesis 8-9

Notes

8.

WIN-WIN SITUATION

Humble yourselves, therefore, under the mighty hand of God, so that
He may exalt you at the proper time.
1 Peter 5:6

During the 2012 Summer Olympics, the world watched as U.S. athlete Gabby Douglas claimed gold in the all-around portion of the gymnastics competition after anchoring the team's run to a gold medal two nights before.

When interviewed immediately after the competition, Douglas flashed her trademark smile, then displayed a depth of maturity rarely seen, "I give all the glory to God. It's kind of a win-win situation. The glory goes up to Him, and the blessings fall down on me."[4]

Douglas's remarks reflect the humility found in another young person who lived years ago. In 1 Kings 3, after Solomon was coronated, God appeared to him in a dream and said, "Ask. What should I give you?" Solomon thanked Him for His faithful love to David, then humbly asked for an obedient heart and discernment (verse 9).

His response pleased the Lord so much, God granted his request, and gave him riches and honor because he did not ask for it. Solomon was the recipient of God's win-win. God received the glory, and His blessings fell upon Solomon.

With her succinct statement, Douglas summarized what true humility is all about. Humility is a combination of several things:

> It opposes false pride,
> focuses on putting others before yourself,
> and displays meekness, modesty and a form of submission.

Humility is never false modesty. True humility can recognize the greatness of a moment but always attributes that greatness to God, not to self. As Peter wrote in today's verse, we should be humble before the Lord. The result? James says if you "humble yourselves before the Lord...He will exalt you." (James 4:10)

When we practice true humility, God not only gets the glory, but, in His great love, He lifts us up. As Douglas reminded us in 2012, all His blessings fall down on us. During our competition, let's remember to be true to God, submit to Him, and give Him Glory. He will lift you up in due time!

Questions

1. Have you ever had a moment of greatness (great achievement, personal best, key victory, won a championship)? What were your thoughts in that moment?

2. How do you display humility during a great moment, when others seek to praise themselves? How do you practice humility on a daily basis?

Further Reading

James 4:6-10, 1 Kings 3 (Solomon's story)

Notes

9.

MASTERING THE ORDINARY

And He was saying to them all, "If anyone wishes to come after Me, he must deny himself, and take up his cross daily and follow Me."
Luke 9:23

So often, as athletes, we dream of making the extraordinary play: taking the last-second shot, making the game-clinching goal, delivering the critical play that seals the victory. In preparing my athletes for success, I encourage them to visualize the execution of our plan at the critical moment. However, we must not forget the reality of sports. In order to be ready for that extraordinary moment, we have to master the ordinary.

Great athletes are made in the off-season, on the practice field, and in the early mornings when no one is watching. When we hear the back-stories of great athletes, the recurring theme is the diligence they applied in the daily grind taking care of the ordinary, daily duties necessary to be at their best when the game was on the line.

One of my favorite coaching stories is from John Wooden. He spent hours training his athletes on the mundane, such as tying their shoes. It was paramount to Wooden that his players always embrace the daily routine. He knew if his team ever hoped to rise to the challenges they faced in competition, they had to be exceptional in the ordinary.

Wooden's training echoed the lesson Christ taught his disciples in Luke 9. After the miraculous feeding of the

5,000, Christ drew his disciples away to pray and addressed them privately. After this public display of His power, He reminded them in Luke 9:23 that being true followers was a daily exercise of setting aside their own agendas and ambitions in their devotion to God.

As Oswald Chambers reminds us, "It is inbred in us that we have to do exceptional things for God; but we have not. We have to be exceptional in the ordinary things, to be holy in mean streets, among mean people, and this is not learned in five minutes."[5]

In my personal life, I was not challenged to structure my morning routine until I was already in ministry. I first read Chambers' quote during this time in my life, and it was an eye-opener. As I sought to be more intentional in my daily habits, I learned that adding a prayer for guidance was no different than tying my shoes, and scripture reading needed a plan to follow on a daily basis. Such simple, mundane steps can have profound results in our lives.

So how are you doing in the little, ordinary decisions of daily life? Are you making daily habits of living as Christ's disciples? If not, then start today and shift your focus to the simple things in life that need refinement. Only then will you be prepared for greatness for God and your sport.

Questions

1. As an athlete or coach, how can you maximize the opportunities to grow and improve during the off-season?

2. List a few areas in your daily Christian walk that could use more practice. How can you work to improve these seemingly "ordinary" attributes?

Further Reading

Proverbs 12:27; Proverbs 6:6-8; 1 Timothy 4:14-16

Notes

10.

FORWARD PROGRESS

The end of a matter is better than its beginning;
Patience of spirit is better than haughtiness of spirit.
Ecclesiastes 7:8

Back when I was a track athlete, I was blessed to have great coaches who taught me about the need for perseverance and patience throughout the track season. My high school coach used to tell me in meets early in the season, "Right now, you are racing against the clock. Try to be a step faster, and you're winning. Remember, the race that matters most is the final in League Championships."

My coach understood the big picture and our goals for the season. He sought to build that same sense into me as well so that I could continue progressing and improving each day to reach the ultimate goal.

Now that I'm a coach myself (women's volleyball), I have reflected on this lesson often. Many times, athletes get lost in the moment and can't see the big picture. Yes, every match matters; every time we step onto the field/floor/track, we should give our best.

But we also need to recognize that we don't want to "peak" too soon. As coaches, we are better equipped to understand the big picture, and we seek to help our athletes progress so that they can peak in the postseason.

In fact, in the best season I've ever had as a coach, my team lost 14 times in the regular season. We lost our conference championship and the regional semifinals, but we were invited to the national tournament as an at-large bid. My players saved their best play for last, pushing through the national tournament and finishing their campaign in the NCCAA National Championships Final Four.

Anyone who followed that team won't remember those losses as much as the postseason success. That team will be remembered for a strong finish to a great season.

The writer of Ecclesiastes understood the concept of process and perseverance. As he neared the end of his life, he reflected on the vanity of life and the wisdom he attained through trial and error. In Ecclesiastes 7:8, he wrote, "The end of a matter is better than its beginning; a patient spirit is better than a proud spirit." And if we look at the New Testament, we find that Paul addressed the issue as well.

Paul gave many calls to persevere, even challenging his protégé Timothy to finish strong in his ministry (1 Tim. 4). Scripture challenges us daily to continue progressing forward, seeking each day to become more Christ-like in our living and our attitude. The challenge, much like the ones we face in our athletic season, is to keep the big picture in mind and to live our daily lives with an eternal perspective.

Hebrews 12:1-3 challenges us to keep our eyes on Jesus, the source and perfecter of our faith. If we consider all that Christ has already accomplished on our behalf and the promises in store for us if we persevere, we will not lose heart!

Questions

1. In your athletic career what steps have you or your team taken to recover from an unexpected or disheartening loss?
2. What do you have in place in your personal life to help you keep the big picture in mind, regardless of high or low points you may face?

Further Reading

Ecclesiastes 3:1-11; Philippians 3:7-16; 2 Timothy 4:7-8

Notes

11.

DESIRE

O LORD, You have heard the desire of the humble;
You will strengthen their heart, You will incline Your ear.
Psalm 10:17

William "Bill" Shoemaker (1931-2003) was a famous American jockey noted for his 11 Triple Crown victories during his career. His accomplishments on the track led to his induction into the American Horse Racing Hall of Fame. A popular quote attributed to Shoemaker states, "Desire is the most important factor in the success of any athlete."[6]

I believe Shoemaker is correct that success in athletics must begin with a deep desire. Why else would we put ourselves through the pain and agony of intense training, the discipline and focus of honing our technique? Why else would we spend hours upon hours studying our particular game? Is it not desire that causes great athletes to dig deep and find a way to win?

In today's text, the Hebrew word *ta'avah* is translated "desire." Its definition in Strong's Lexicon reads, "desire, wish, longings of one's heart."[7]

I believe there is a two-fold message within this word for us as Christians. Today, let's focus on how this word affects us individually.

In our Christian literature, desire many times is associated negatively with the flesh...but the Bible also uses the word

34

in a positive light: In a different Bible translation, the psalmist wrote, "One thing I have desired...that I may dwell in the house of the Lord...to behold the beauty of the Lord and inquire in His temple." (Psalm 27:4, NKJV).

The Hebrew word *sha'al* is translated "desire" in this version. It is also translated "inquired," or "asked."[8] As the psalmist progresses through this particular psalm, he paints the picture of someone who inquires of the Lord out of his longing to be with Him. Many other scriptures point toward the inner desire to love God and to serve Him with all that we are.

So what is your desire? Is it solely for earthly victories and the spoils that go to the victor? Or do you desire eternal victory, which can only be found in the ONE who overcame all, Jesus Christ? Is Jesus truly the ONE object of your desire...or do other, minor longings replace that desire to follow him? Are you focused on Christ with a single-minded intent, to serve Him with all that you are?

If so, then I agree with Shoemaker...you have found the secret to live life victoriously.

Questions

1. Why do you think desire is a key character quality to be a champion?
2. How can desire direct you in your daily walk with God?

Further Reading

Psalm 27:4-14; Philippians 3:8-14

Notes

12.

SPREADING THE SALT

You are the salt of the earth. But if the salt loses its saltiness, how can it be made salty again? It is no longer good for anything, except to be thrown out and trampled underfoot by men.
Matthew 5:13

Moments after his wonderful victory at the 2007 Masters, an emotional Zach Johnson was asked by a reporter what he carried within him that helped him sustain his lead in the final round. He replied, "My Christian faith is very important to me. It was very special to win the Masters golf tournament on Easter Sunday. I'm very blessed. I would like to thank God. I felt Jesus Christ with me on the golf course every step of the way."[9]

In the exuberance and celebration following his momentous victory, Johnson could have exulted in his play. Instead, Johnson's desire for God was evident in his speech and actions. His personal testimony of faith was widely ignored by the media, but many Christians watching that live interview were inspired by his words and his faith.

Our own personal desire to love and serve the Lord will keep us in His game-plan...but how will our desire inspire others to stay in His game plan? If we are seeking to fulfill Christ's Great Commission, then our actions should have a specific result. We should see others hunger for God's goodness and thirst for the things of heaven.

37

If we investigated the different relationships Christ cultivated with sinners, we'd find He always stirred within them a desire to know more, to want more.

> "Sir give me this water so that I won't get thirsty." (John 4:15)
> "How can one be born again?" (John 3:4)

In His encounters, Jesus set people on a quest to obtain what He offered…eternal life. His life is an example of how we should live, and today's scripture challenges us to remain "salty."

How do we live as "salt of the earth"? I believe we become salt when everything about our lives permeates the love and grace of God. Whether it is our efforts on the floor that cause our opponents to gain respect for us, or an act of kindness with an encouraging word to a stranger…or something else…we should 'rub off' on those around us.

We should leave a little of ourselves with them. We should leave an impression – and that impression should be Christ…and hopefully, we will have set that person further on their quest for God.

Questions

1. As an athlete or coach, what did others see in your actions and attitude that is different? Did those actions point toward Christ?
2. What would change if you intentionally align your actions to be pleasing to God? Would anyone notice a difference?

Further Reading

John 4:1-30; John 3:1-18; Acts 17:22-32

Notes

13.

IT'S ALL ABOUT HEART

Man looks at the outward appearance,
but the LORD looks at the heart.
1 Samuel 16:7b

In 2008, Stephen Curry torched teams in the first three rounds of the NCAA basketball tournament averaging 34.3 points per game and leading his team to their first Regional Championship since 1969. Though Kansas outlasted Curry and the tenacious Davidson team to advance to the Final Four, the Davidson Wildcats would go down in the history books as the Cinderella team of 2008.

As a high school prospect, Curry was overlooked by several teams that had ended their seasons long before that tournament. He was a scrawny 6'1" 155-pound senior, considered too small and frail to handle the physical play in the AAC and SEC.

Many major Division I coaches could not get past his physique…but one coach looked beneath the skin. Coach Bob Mckillop saw something in the slender shooter from Charlotte Christian – he saw the heart of a champion and took a risk. As the sports world discovered that March in 2008, that risk has paid off.

Curry understands that with man, things may appear impossible, but nothing is impossible with God – in fact, on his shoes he has "4:13" written in black ink, a reference to one of his favorite Bible verses, Philippians 4:13. Curry provided fans with many shining moments during the 2008 tournament. His quiet calm in the midst of the battle is a reminder to us that God has a purpose for each of us. His story reminds me of another young man who was overlooked years ago.

In 1 Samuel 16, Samuel was commissioned by God to go and anoint the second king of Israel. He was led to the home of Jesse of Bethlehem, where God said he would find the one whom God Himself had chosen. When Samuel looked upon Eliab, he said, "surely the Lord's anointed is before Him!"

God told Samuel, "Do not look at his appearance or at the height of his stature, because I have rejected him; for God sees not as man sees, for man looks at the outward appearance, but the Lord looks at the heart" (1 Samuel 16: 7). Eventually, the youngest son was brought before him, and the Lord instructed Samuel to anoint him.

Sometime later, as David stood over the defeated body of Goliath, I can imagine Samuel must have felt the same confirmation in his heart that Coach McKillop felt seeing Curry lead Davidson deep into 2008's tournament.

Let's remember that "God has chosen the weak things of the world to shame the things which are strong" (1 Corinthians 1:27). As David said before he slew Goliath, "all…may know that the Lord does not deliver by sword or by spear; for the *battle* is the Lord's" (1 Samuel 17:47, emphasis added).

Questions

1. In your sport, what are the qualities of an athlete who competes with "heart"?
2. What indicators do you see in your life that God is fulfilling His purpose in and through you?

Further Reading

Nehemiah 4:6; Romans 1:16; 1 Corinthians 1:28-31

Notes

14.

ORDER MY STEPS:
THE RIGHT DIRECTION

*Your word is a lamp to my feet and a light to my path. Establish my
footsteps in Your word, and do not let any iniquity
have dominion over me.*
Psalm 119: 105, 133

Former Olympic Speed-skater Chad Hedrick won five
Olympic medals during his racing career. In the 2010
Vancouver Winter Olympics, he earned his final medal in
the 1000 meters. He is considered one of the most
prominent figures in Olympic Speed-skating history.
Haven Today broadcast an interview with Hedrick on
February 18, 2010. The key line of the intro was "Chad
Hedrick is not the same Chad Hedrick of four years ago."[10]

During that interview, Hedrick discussed his recent
conversion experience. He admitted that most people knew
him as a guy that worked hard and played hard. In
describing his commitment to Christ, he said, "Now I find
myself...really living a Godly life now. *I feel like I'm going in
the right direction.*"

In today's passage, the psalmist expressed his devotion to
God and the highest regard toward scripture by using the
letters of the Hebrew alphabet to begin each stanza. His
words, "establish my footsteps," remind me of a training
session I had years ago with a developing athlete. She was

learning the footwork to run a specific attack, and I was speaking with her parents about the proper footwork. Her mother joked, "maybe you can put those images of steps on the floor so she knows exactly where to step, like they do in dancing!" It was an insignificant moment, but I reflected on that dialogue when I heard Chad's interview later.

Chad took a hard look at his life and decided to go a different direction from his previous path. He found Christ to be the answer to his life-questions and decided to trust his life to Christ. In that decision, he chose to follow Christ's path for him.

As athletes, we submit to a coach because we believe he or she will guide us to succeed. We learn techniques, mechanics, and plays to help us achieve that success. But do we consistently give Christ that same devotion?

The Bible, God's Word, is not a 'fix-all' book. It is not a book of do's and don'ts. It is not just a history book. It is God's love letter to us and His testament to us. Through the Bible and the power of the Holy Spirit, we are equipped, complete in *every* way (2 Timothy 3:16). More than that, through it God reveals *His* game-plan for the world, and *His* plan for us!

Trust Christ, then take the next step. Trust His Word, stand on His promises, and let it light your paths.

Questions

1.   As an athlete, do you recall an experience where you disagreed with your coach, but chose to submit to his or her instructions? What was the result?
2.   List some 'little steps' you can put in place to ensure you stay on the right path daily.

Further Reading
Psalm 119; Proverbs 16:9; 2 Thessalonians 3:5

Notes

15.

STICK TO THE PLAN

The end of all things is near; therefore, be of sound judgment and sober spirit for the purpose of prayer. Above all, keep fervent in your love for one another, because love covers a multitude of sins. Be hospitable to one another without complaint. As each one has received a special gift, employ it in serving one another as good stewards of the manifold grace of God. Whoever speaks, is to do so as one who is speaking the utterances of God; whoever serves is to do so as one who is serving by the strength which God supplies; so that in all things God may be glorified through Jesus Christ, to whom belongs the glory and dominion forever and ever. Amen.
1 Peter 4:7-11

I love March Madness! I grew up playing basketball, played the game until I was in high school, and supported my older brother through his college career. I coached the game for a number of years as well. To me, nothing beats the passion, desire, and determination these collegiate young men and women display during the "Big Dance."

At the conclusion of the Elite 8 round in 2007, Ohio State, UCLA, Florida and Georgetown overcame large deficits to advance to the next round. The poise the teams displayed down the stretch was discussed by commentators and fans following the tournament.

When teams are equally matched, something has to give. In my coaching circle, we like to say, "The loser will be the team that blinks first." Throughout these matches, there were great plays, great coaching moves, and great runs, but what separated these teams from the pack is at the core of every great team; the teams that prevailed that weekend were clear-headed, focused, and stuck to their coach's plan.

In the midst of the battle, winners are clear-headed. They remember the basics. They stick to the fundamentals. They remember WHO they are, and from where they have come. These four teams (Ohio State, UCLA, Florida, and Georgetown) understood one particular phrase expressed by coaches when the pressure is on: "this is our chance, we win or go home. Trust each other, stay under control, and *stick to the game plan*! We will prevail in the end!"

In today's scripture, Peter writes with passion and urgency declaring, "The end of all things is near!" Peter, as he wrote, must have pictured that fateful night with Jesus before the crucifixion. Christ spent his final night before he was betrayed preparing the disciples for their ministry.

In these verses, Peter echoes what Jesus said that night as he gives instruction to the church on how they should live. Yet I believe it is important that Peter opened this passage with the phrase; "therefore, be of sound judgment and sober *spirit* for the purpose of prayer."

We live in the last days, and do not know when Christ will return. Let's be clear-headed and disciplined for prayer. Let's remember who we are, and *whose* we are, and let's get on the battlefield. The game-plan is sure, the victory is secure. We will prevail if we stick to the plan!

Questions

1. In a tightly contested match, what are some keys to sticking to a game plan?
2. What are 2-3 steps you need to take to stick to Christ's plan for you?

Further Reading
John 13-17; 1 Peter 2

Notes

16.

DEFINING MOMENTS

If it is disagreeable in your sight to serve the LORD, choose for
yourselves today whom you will serve: whether the gods which your
fathers served which were beyond the River, or the gods of the Amorites
in whose land you are living; but as for me and my house,
we will serve the LORD.
Joshua 24:15

In 2011, the college basketball world was abuzz at the Final Four, and filled with a number of main storylines: VCU and their improbable run, Butler's incredible two-year dominance, UConn's amazing postseason string, and Kentucky's resilience. As story after story emerged about each team and their journey, members of each squad discussed their season's defining moments.

UConn won the national championship after finishing ninth in their conference with a 9-9 record and then achieving an 11-game run through conference championships and the NCAA tournament.

In looking back at that tournament, I quietly wonder what shaped those teams. What molded them into the team they became? Was it a decision they reached together? Was it a particular moment in a certain game? Did the coaches make a change that brought the team together?

Regardless of the reason, most commentators are clear about one thing: each team had a defining moment that shaped the outcome of their season.

In Scripture, we read about one such moment in the life of Joshua. Many would say it was during his campaign to take the land of Canaan, but I think it began back in Numbers 13. Moses sent one man from each of the 12 tribes to scout the land of Canaan. Among those 12 were two young men named Joshua and Caleb. After the spies had investigated the land, they returned bringing a dismal report to Moses.

The people of Israel broke into an uproar, crying and fearful. Israel rebelled against God's command to take the land. Joshua and Caleb, however, tore their garments and proclaimed, "The land we passed through and explored is exceedingly good. If the LORD is pleased with us, he will lead us into that land, a land flowing with milk and honey, and will give it to us. Only do not rebel against the LORD. And do not be afraid of the people of the land, because we will devour them. Their protection is gone, but the LORD is with us. Do not be afraid of them" (Numbers 14:7-9).

In that moment, God honored these two young men. Although He brought calamity on Israel, He allowed these two spies to survive the 40 years in the wilderness and cross into the promised land.

Just like Joshua, we will all face a moment in our lives when we will have to make a major choice, and that choice may define who we will become. Howard T. Dickens Jr. has been quoted as saying, "If we don't decide to step out of our box—come out of our comfort zone—we won't progress and live beyond our present potential, but regress and remain in the reality of our own limitation."[11]

VCU, Butler, Kentucky and UConn enjoyed the results of the choices they made when they faced their defining moments. Joshua and Caleb were allowed to enter Canaan because they faced their defining moment and "stepped outside of the box." On the flipside, an entire generation of Israel failed to realize their potential as the people of God and failed to receive the power of God when they didn't step up.

Today, when your moment comes, face it with eternity in sight. Trust Christ, the author and finisher of your race, to strengthen you to make the right choice and take a stand. Let your decision be God's decision and allow it to define who you will become according to His perfect plan!

Questions

1. To this point in your athletic life, what has been your most defining moment?
2. What is the single-most important moment or conversation in your Christian walk that dramatically changed your life?

Further Reading

1 Samuel 15-17

Notes

17.

WHATEVER YOU DO, DO HEARTILY

Whatever you do, do your work heartily, as for the Lord rather than for men, knowing that from the Lord you will receive the reward of the inheritance. It is the Lord Christ whom you serve.
Colossians 3:23-24

Why do we play sports? What is our priority? For whom are we playing? These are questions we each struggle with as players and as coaches.

If we search our souls, I believe that we each desire to win and that we each play for some personal reason beyond "the team," whether it be for personal glory, personal gratification, etc.
But when we gather together to play as a team, those who thrive have the ability to do two things:

> 1) put aside their personal goals and priorities, and
> 2) align themselves with team priorities.

Great team victories have been achieved by groups of individuals who determined their priorities and submitted to their team goals.

In 1992, I lost my volleyball stat-girl (who was also my starting point guard) in a horrific, mid-season car accident. My volleyball team and the football team chose to dedicate the remainder of their seasons to her. The football team, a fledgling first-year, 8-man program, had not won a game yet. The next two games they played were their best of the season, even though the team did not win.

53

Our volleyball team, which was 2-2 at that point, went on a 15-match winning streak, which carried the team into sectional playoffs. The teams were unified for one purpose: they set aside their personal ambitions and dedicated their seasons to honor their fallen fellow. As one player noted in a team huddle, "whatever I do will be to honor Amber."

I firmly believe our challenge as Christians is to take today's verse for what it is. Sometimes we over-analyze scripture, and miss the simple, yet profound challenge for us. Paul did not say, "*If* you work in a certain field, do it unto the Lord." He said, "Whatever!"

This grants us the freedom to take our sport and dedicate ourselves to excellence. If Christ is our priority, and He is truly at the center of our lives, then play *for Him*!

Regardless of the score; regardless of the outcome on the scoreboard or in the wins column, play for Christ and Christ alone! We should align our dreams and goals so that our efforts will be pleasing unto Him; because ultimately, He is the one who will reward you.

One statement from my current player handbook reads: "If you receive All-Conference, All-Region or All-American status, we will celebrate. . .but demonstrate the same level of personal excellence on and off the court. . .then we feel we are truly blessed--and you will too, because your efforts will be pleasing unto the Lord."

If we each are doing our 'whatever' with determination, dedication and discipline, we will do well. If we are playing with an attitude that says, "My utmost for His highest," I believe God is pleased; and just like a proud, loving father,

He beams in the stands when you leave your all on the floor.

But let's take this a step farther. Let's make sure that every element of our lives is lived with that same passion we bring to our sport. When we do so, I am convinced we will hear those words children long to hear from their father, "Well done."

Questions

1. What are some critical steps you have taken as an athlete in order to align with a team's plan?
2. When you look at the priorities in your personal life - the 4-5 areas of your life where you spend the most time and energy - what steps are you taking to ensure you apply yourself daily with all that you have to offer?

Further Reading

1 Corinthians 10:31; Philippians 1:27; Colossians 3:17

Notes

18.

HOME CROWD: CLOUD OF WITNESSES

Therefore, since we have so great a cloud of witnesses surrounding us, let us also lay aside every encumbrance and the sin which so easily entangles us, and let us run with endurance the race that is set before us, fixing our eyes on Jesus, the author and perfecter of faith, who for the joy set before Him endured the cross, despising the shame, and has sat down at the right hand of the throne of God. For consider Him who has endured such hostility by sinners against Himself, so that you will not grow weary and lose heart.
Hebrews 12:1-3

For an athlete, there is nothing like competing in front of a home crowd, nothing more inspiring than hearing the cheers, feeling the energy, and responding to the wave of encouragement. In 2012, 24 year old U.S. Decathlete Ashton Eaton rode the cheers of his home crowd to a remarkable accomplishment at the US Olympic Trials.

During the 2-day 10-event competition, Eaton set two world decathlon records in the 100 meters and the long jump, but needed one more personal best in the final event, the grueling 1500 meters, to break the world record in the decathlon.

Eaton, a strong runner, ran the four laps to a crowd on its feet – the noise level was palpable as the crowd cheered him on. Despite the fatigue from 48 grueling hours of competition, Eaton had a marvelous finish, accentuated by the 1st place runner surrendering his lead to allow Ashton the full, sweet taste of victory as he surged past the second-place runner.

Immediately after crossing the line, Eaton burst into tears and fell into the arms of his fiancée and his mother as the crowd burst anew, the full realization sinking in that this young man had established a new world record in the event, setting a new standard as the "World's Best Athlete." The brotherhood of decathletes quickly circled him, congratulating him, and former world decathlete Dan O'Brien came out of the crowd to give him a hug.

Eaton's victory is a special reminder to us as Christians that we never run our race alone. As we face the daily challenges of life in a world tainted by sin, we can know that we are surrounded by many who have run this race before us, and many who ran alongside.

Just as Eaton had to overcome each obstacle that stood between him and a Decathlon world record, we must face each obstacle that comes before us. Each obstacle holds its own challenge, yet scripture says that we *can* throw off everything that entangles us.

As we trust Christ in each situation, we find strength in Him, but we also find strength in the company of others who uplift us, intercede for us, and encourage us. "Go on," they cry, "finish the race!"

When asked how he felt after finishing his race, Eaton exclaimed, "there's really very few words you can say that describe this!"[12] We, too, will have an indescribable feeling when we finish our race and see Jesus, the author and perfecter of our faith, standing at the line with His arms open. Since we have such a great crowd of witnesses and we serve a mighty God, let's run and not grow weary, let's walk and not grow faint!

Questions

1. What obstacles might you have to overcome to achieve a memorable victory before your home crowd?
2. What preventative steps can you put in place to overcome obstacles in your daily walk with Christ?

Further Reading
Hebrews 11:32-40

Notes

19.

PRIDE IS A TEAM-KILLER

Pride goes before destruction,
And a haughty spirit before stumbling.
Proverbs 16:18

During the 2010 World Cup Soccer Championships, the world watched as a proud French team melted down – not in a match against a worthy opponent, but on the training field as infighting led to a team boycott.

Though this was only the final public scene of an ongoing feud, the boycott appeared as a group of arrogant players, who felt they knew more than the coaching staff and administration. Their prideful conduct was condemned by the soccer community.

Whether one player thinks he is better than his coach or a team believes they are superior to their opponent, Pride is a *team-killer*. At the high school, college, and club level, I have watched pride destroy great work.

One club volleyball season, I was blessed with an over-achieving team that made a great run to the region championship match. With a bid for a national tournament on the line, the team had a melt-down. Why?

Because of pride and self-centered attitudes. One player used her position to not support another. As the second player realized what was happening, an argument ensued, and I was left trying to quickly get the individuals back on the same page from the sideline while the team struggled without two of its critical players. Of course, the team lost the critical match and their opportunity to advance to the national tournament.

Isaiah 14:12-17 tells us about the pride of one being, naming him Lucifer. The Lord's creation thought he was better than the Creator! Revelation describes through metaphor and prophecy the details of Lucifer's arrogant march on God's throne and his fall from heaven. It is easy to see the arrogance and pride of Lucifer...but how many of us carry a haughty spirit in our hearts?

When we begin to think of ourselves as more than we ought, we find ourselves in league with Lucifer. Scripture warns us constantly that pride will bring us down. We will cause strife and destroy the unity and sanctity of our team.

Pride is a condition that will destroy your team. It will also destroy your walk with God. Your pride will be your downfall. James 4:10 tells us to humble ourselves, and *God* will lift us up!

Questions

1. How does pride tear apart team unity?
2. What examples does Christ give us regarding pride and humility?

Further Reading

Proverbs 13:10; Proverbs 29:23; Proverbs 28:25;
James 4:6-10

Notes

20.

An Expensive Mistake

Your word I have treasured in my heart,
That I may not sin against You.
Psalm 119:11

The 2010 Winter Olympics provided many wonderful, heartwarming stories about overcoming obstacles and having great perseverance. Sadly, we also were given a few painful life lessons as well.

One of them involved the Netherlands' Sven Kramer, arguably the greatest long-distance speed skater in the world at the time. One evening, as he was on his way to setting a world record in the 10,000-meters, something went wrong.

It seemed he had skated eight laps in the wrong lane. The video replay revealed a confused Kramer being told by his coach to change lanes, which he eventually did. However, his coach had been mistaken; Kramer was in the correct lane at the time. The mistake cost him a gold medal and a world record performance.

In a televised interview later that evening, Kramer said, "This really sucks. This is a real expensive mistake."[13]

As heart-wrenching as it was to see this mistake made on such a public stage, Kramer's humility really moved me. His words struck me as very similar to another man, who had been known as one of the greatest kings of all time: David.

Most of us are familiar with David's story and his notable shortcomings, one of which was his adultery with Bathsheba and the resulting murder of her husband, Uriah. However, what we fail to recognize is that this sinful turn in his life began before he saw Bathsheba on the roof-top.

In 2 Samuel 11, David sent his men to battle, but did not proceed with them. Perhaps he was tired of war or was dealing with something urgent.

Regardless, he didn't take his normal position at the head of his army in leading them to besiege the Ammonite capital of Rabbah.

This seemingly benign decision meant that he was home the night he saw Bathsheba instead of out with his troops.

From that little decision to stay home came a landslide of adultery, lies, cover-up, and murder. Later, one of David's friends confronted him and he admitted his sin. End of story, right? Wrong.

First, the son born to David and Bathsheba died. Then we read of the consequences of his actions as his son defiled a daughter, another son killed that one and eventually sought to abdicate the throne only to die in a shameful manner. David's family is decimated because of a little, yet expensive, mistake.

Through David's story, we can be reminded that we are just as susceptible to mistakes, errors and sin. It also reminds us that, though we are forgiven of our sins if we confess them, we can still accumulate horrible earthly consequences for our actions.

We are given one life to serve God and love others. We need to learn from the mistakes of others and learn that our mistakes have consequences on this earth. As we enter new seasons in life, I exhort you to follow the words of the Psalmist.

Hide God's word in your heart so that when that moment comes, and you have a choice to make, you will hear God speaking to you and make a wise decision. Stay on the side of right, and you will be truly blessed. Don't take that drink from a friend, don't go to that party to "fit in," don't give in to pressure to "show your love." The consequences may be far greater than you can imagine.

Questions

1. Do you recall a time when you or a teammate made a poor choice that negatively affected your team?

2. How do you prepare for the tough decisions in your life, so that you can make a choice for righteousness? (e.g. Do I take the drink? Do I go to this party? Do I let my friend drive?)

Further Reading

2 Samuel 11-19; Psalm 51

Notes

21.

GETTING BACK ON THE RIGHT PATH

And we know that God causes all things to work together for good to those who love God, to those who are called according to His purpose.
Romans 8:28

When I was 16, I was a young, brash 3-sport athlete who took any challenge that came my way. My aggressive personality allowed me to "hang with the big-dawgs" on the court, in the field, or on the track. However, my personality also caused many setbacks.

I was attending a summer camp that year. During one break, I nonchalantly leapt off a small hill as some of the campers were goofing off. One of my friends dared me to try the same feat off a larger hill. Not one to back down from a challenge, I promptly went to the top, backed up, took a few steps, and jumped.

The exhilaration of flying lasts for a few seconds. The excitement of meeting the challenge lasted just as long...until I hit the ground. I knew I had done something seriously wrong when I hit the ground.

My leg turned outward upon impact, and I severely injured my leg. Later in the emergency room, the ER doctor told me it looked like I had been in a car accident: torn ligaments, cartilage, and broken bones. That one moment was my expensive mistake...and the consequences were far-reaching.

I lost any opportunity to earn a scholarship in the sport I loved the most. I also had to walk away from the competitive component of my second sport – one which I had played since the age of 5. I spent 4 months in a cast, another two in a brace, 4 months doing rehab, and suffered through a painful track season the next spring.

To say the least, it was a humbling experience – I had no one to blame but myself and had to acknowledge my own reckless decision. I also was reminded time and again that I needed to learn from what I had done.

God did not spare me the consequences for my choice. However, He did turn it into an opportunity to set me on a career path. You see, the parent of a friend was the director of the local youth basketball league. He came to me during the fall and asked if I wanted to coach. I was at first reluctant, but he informed me I would get to coach my little brother's team. I tried it and had an enjoyable experience.

The next year I committed to coach again, this time leading an 8th grade team, and found a new direction in my life. God kick-started a 20+ year coaching career that began as a sidebar to an expensive mistake in my personal life. He has allowed me to experience championships, personal honors, and players' honors over that span. He has also given me the privilege of touching the lives of people in a way that I could not as a player.

God is seeking to give us His best. If we humble ourselves before Him and acknowledge the errors of our ways, He will still use us. Much like a dirty glass is cleansed in the dishwasher, He promises in 1 John 1:9 to cleanse us of all unrighteousness and make us useful again for His purposes.

In 2 Samuel 12, David did eventually see something positive come forth in the aftermath of his sin. God did not desert him in the aftermath. After the death of Bathsheba's child, God gave them Solomon, who would finish the temple and become one of the greatest kings of Israel.

Perhaps you have already committed some act that you regret. Acknowledge your behavior and actions as wrong in God's eyes and accept His forgiveness. Accept whatever earthly consequences may come…but do not count yourself as useless for His services. God is still God, still loves you, and still has a plan for you. If you humble yourself, He *will* lift you up. He'll set you back on your feet and set you on the right path.

Questions

1. How have you seen a tough circumstance or decision in your sports life create a growth opportunity for you?
2. What steps can you take to turn a difficult circumstance or mistake into an opportunity to grow stronger in your faith?

Further Reading

2 Samuel 11-12; Psalm 51; 1 John 1:9

Notes

22.

WORDS OF GRACE

Let no unwholesome word proceed from your mouth, but only such a word as is good for edification according to the need of the moment, so that it will give grace to those who hear.
Ephesians 4:29

During my tenure at Bryan College, I had the privilege of coordinating our college baseball team's tournament and working with some great coaches and teams. The weekend was very competitive, and the teams showed great character as they battled for the prize of "tournament champion."

As I watched the competitions, I found myself observing the coaching of one particular coach, Dr. Aaron Brister - the head coach at Emmanuel College. Brister has been involved in baseball for a long time; he turned down numerous baseball offers after finishing at Harding University including a minor league contract with the Atlanta Braves. While completing his Ph.D., Brister worked as a full-time youth pastor. His pastoring skills were evident in his coaching.

Time and again, I watched as he lifted up the spirits of his young men. He was a constant voice of encouragement: "Great job, #19! Atta Boy, #25! That's the way to stick to the plan!" As I watched him, I could see a look in his young players' eyes...a look of confidence, loyalty, and of gratitude.
In the heat of battle, these young men were not harangued for mistakes; they were not dressed down for errors on the

field. No, instead, they were built up, edified for the need of the moment, propped up to finish the job at hand.

His inspirational coaching led their team to the tournament championship match. Even though they lost in the championship, I know those men felt good about their accomplishments.

I was inspired as well, because Coach Brister exemplified Ephesians 4:29 and reminded me that, as a coach, I have a direct impact on my players' lives. I am reminded of a powerful and popular passage attributed to Haim Ginott which I read some years ago.

Over time, I changed the words from the original to fit the context of a coach:

> Concerning a *coach's* influence, I have come to the frightening conclusion that I am the decisive element on the *court/field*. It's my personal approach that creates the climate. It's my daily mood that makes the weather. As a *coach*, I possess a tremendous power to make a *player's* life miserable or joyous. I can be a tool of torture or an instrument of inspiration. I can humiliate or heal. In all situations, it is my response that decides whether a crisis will be escalated or de-escalated, and a *player* humanized or dehumanized.[14]

God has placed us in an honorable field. Let us be intentional in living out Ephesians 4:29, bringing grace to those who hear. Let's remember our calling, live up to the challenge, and uplift our players and teammates. Our words will leave an impression that could last for eternity.

Questions

1. How do you handle pressure moments in a game? Do you allow a moment of disappointment, anger, frustration, or approval tear apart months of work, just so we can "vent" and feel justified?
2. What steps can you take to handle moments of pressure in a Godly way?

Further Reading

2 Chronicles 32:6-8; Proverbs 16:24; James 1:19; Luke 6:31

Notes

23.

TWO ARE BETTER THAN ONE

Two are better than one,
because they have a good return for their labor.
Ecclesiastes 4:9

In October 2007, Jeff Gordon pulled off a masterful victory in the UAW-Ford 500, without ever holding a lead until the final lap. The brilliant run by Gordon and his Hendrick Motorsports' teammate Jimmie Johnson actually began at the back of the pack, waiting to make their run for the "Big One," the seemingly usual multi-car wreck at this Talladega track.

Late in the race, Gordon and Johnson found themselves in the middle of a large front-running pack on the speed-friendly track. The pack had worked together in two and sometimes three "drafting" lines to stay in the front, but the lines were breaking up, causing people to lose their objective.

The objective, (in non-driver terms) is for one car to break the wind as the others file in tightly behind, at times physically touching bumpers. The front car pulls the others along, saving their engines some labor, while the cars behind allow a tunnel to form, which pushes the front car…in other words, the group works together to achieve more with less effort.

With just a few laps to go, Johnson began to draft on Gordon, and the team quickly shot to the front. In the post-race interview, Gordon said, "I really thought Jimmie was going to win the race...I didn't think anybody was going to get around him, let alone me."[15]

As the race drew to an end, Gordon sought to pass his teammate, but needed a push from another competitor, Tony Steward. "He drilled me, and he's the one who pushed me up front," Gordon commented. The end result was a 1-2 victory for the teammates, Gordon and Johnson — two are better than one!

We need to apply this unique example of teamwork to our lives. We were not created to live life in a vacuum. We were created to be interdependent with each other as we serve the Lord. At times, we are to push each other, and sometimes we need to be pushed, to get us on track in our lives. Other times, we need to "take the lead' to lighten the load for those coming alongside us.

The result is, we ALL reach the finish line, where our Lord will say to us, "Well done!" Two are better than one — for they will have a good return for their work.

Questions

1. Can you recall a time when you had to respond to a "push" from a teammate or competitor? Describe your response.

2. What are positive ways you can challenge the people God places in your life to grow spiritually in their daily lives?

Further Reading
2 Timothy 1:3-14

Notes

24.

HOPE: EAGER EXPECTATION

And David said, "The LORD who delivered me from the paw of the lion and from the paw of the bear, He will deliver me from the hand of this Philistine."
1 Samuel 17:37

In the opening round of the 2018 NCAA Basketball Championships, UMBC (University of Maryland, Baltimore County), a little known 16th seed did what has never been done before. The little school took down the #1 seed in the tournament, the University of Virginia. The UMBC team dominated the match, and left no doubt that for one particular night, they were the better team. Their accomplishment was historic in nature, and destroyed almost every March Madness Bracket available. The talk of David slaying Goliath was rampant during the early weeks of March thanks to this relatively unknown underdog.

In 1 Samuel 17, we are told of Israel's encounter with Goliath, the great warrior of the Philistines. In the passage, Goliath stepped forward and challenged the Israelites to single combat to decide the battle. The Israelites ran in fear from this warrior who stood over 9 feet tall and was strong as an ox. NBA basketball great Shaquille O'Neal, who stands over 7 feet tall, would be about 18 inches shorter than Goliath, a perfect illustration of the massive size of this man. Little David was undeterred and proclaimed that his God would deliver the Philistine giant into his hands.

Where did David get such confidence? His *hope* was in the Lord. Hope is not simply a personal desire, or wishful thinking, as many define it today. In the Christian life, hope becomes our reality, a natural outcome of belief. A Christian's belief is fixated on the person of God, rooted in the authentic witness of scripture, and centered on the reality of our relationship with Christ. The product of that belief is a confidence in God and a certainty that His plan for us is far better than all that we can ask or imagine.

David also had a history with God. God had delivered the lion and the bear to him, so David could trust God. Because of his history, David had tremendous optimism that God would deliver Goliath into his hands. His optimism was built upon the eternal promise from the Promise-Keeper, which gave David an eager expectation for the great things God would do.

As a coach, I believe my most vital role is to instill hope in my team — hope that we can achieve our goals and hope that we can overcome our obstacles. We use the David/Goliath story any time we know the odds are stacked against our team. It gives the team the confidence that "if it has happened before, maybe today it will happen again." As Christians, though, we rely on more than just wishful thinking. As Romans 5:5 says, "And hope does not disappoint, because the love of God has been poured out within our hearts through the Holy Spirit who was given to us."

As Christians, scripture encourages us to live our lives with eager expectation to our future, and a confidence in God's plan because of what He has done for us. When we do so, we can truly live life with the joy that Christ said will make us complete in Him.

Questions

1. Recall to memory an occasion when you recognized how your training prepared you for competition. How did it instill confidence in you?
2. Take time to recall your walk with the Lord. How has your history with Him inspired you to trust His promises to you?

Further Reading

1 Samuel 17:32-50; Psalm 71:5-6; Romans 4:18-21; Romans 5:1-5

Notes

25.

CHRISTIAN HOPE

*We exult in hope of the glory of God. And not only this, but we also
exult in our tribulations, knowing that tribulation brings about
perseverance; and perseverance, proven character;
and proven character, hope.*
Romans 5:2b-4

Yesterday, we talked about hope. And we used words that
can actually serve as an acronym for the word itself:
H–history, O–optimism, P–Promise, E-Eager Expectation.

Understanding Christian hope can be a great thing. But
what should it produce in us? In the sports world, hope is
necessary in spurring a team to do great things. Without
hope, why would we as athletes endure what we do? If we
cannot achieve our goals, why would we endure the
hardship of preseason training? Why would we waste hours
studying film, learning our skills, pushing our bodies
beyond what we thought possible? Why would we choose
to follow a game-plan if we knew it was going to fail? The
truth for most of us is that we wouldn't.

One of the toughest situations to endure is a long losing
season when there is no hope of turning things around. At
some point, everyone checks out. That is why the team
leaders must be hope-igniters!

Southport High School's (IN) football coach Bill Peebles
developed that sense of hope as he rebuilt the school's
program. He had to rebuild their battered confidence, and it

took three years to do. His promises of future glory paid off in 2008 as the Cardinals finished with their first winning season (9-2) since 1995 and advanced to their state semifinals.

When we have hope, it spurs us to do many things:

H – We are willing to **heed** the words of wisdom from those who have gone before us.

O – It produces **obedience** because we have the confidence that the outcome will be good.

P – It gives us **patience** as we persevere through the temporary hardship.

E – It gives us renewed **energy** to keep working hard.

The hope of the future spurred Paul to keep pressing on when all odds were against him. He challenged the early church to keep pressing on by heeding and obeying God's Word, even in the worst of times. We must do the same. Read the additional passages listed on the following page and be encouraged to keep pressing on. He who began a good work in you will be faithful to complete it until the day of Jesus Christ (Philippians 1:6).

Questions

1. Take the acronym for hope and apply it to your sport. What are examples of H.O.P.E. in your athletic life?
2. How does having a sense of hope help you overcome struggles in your daily life?

Further Reading

Psalm 51:10-13; Romans 5:1-5; Romans 8:18-25; Romans 8:31-39; 2 Corinthians 4:7-10

Notes

26.

DILIGENCE

The plans of the diligent lead surely to advantage,
But everyone who is hasty comes surely to poverty.
Proverbs 21:5

Coach John Wooden (1910-2010), arguably the greatest coach in college basketball, was a man of great wisdom, integrity, and deep faith in God. Wooden, who led the UCLA Bruins to 10 national championships, was known for meticulous attention to detail – his handbook had rules governing hair length, and even the proper etiquette for shoe-tying.

In his book, "Wooden on Leadership," Coach Wooden stated, "Little things make all the difference in the world...'Little things make big things happen' is the phrase I used in pointing out the importance of correct selection and perfection of details."[16] He devotes an entire chapter in his book to the concept of diligence and attention to details.

What is diligence? The Free Dictionary by Farlex defines diligence as "earnest and persistent application to an undertaking; steady effort; assiduity"[17]. The Oxford English Dictionary defines it as "careful and persistent work or effort."[18]

Diligence is one of the greatest intangible qualities of champions. NFL-great Payton Manning is known for his diligence in preparation – each week memorizing not only his offensive sets, but the opponent's defensive sets and cues. Michael Jordan and Larry Bird were known for their 500+ shot game-day shoot-around rituals.

Much of scripture challenges us to be diligent in every detail of our lives. The Hebrew word *shamar*[19] and the Greek word *spoude*[20] are both similarly translated as diligent in the Old and New Testament, meaning to take earnest care, utmost diligence (See scriptures listed in Further Reading).

Do we devote ourselves to the little details of life as much as we do our sport? Many of us "lag in diligence" when it comes to adherence to Christian principles and doctrines. Jesus, the greatest "Coach" of all, is calling you to be diligent so that you may inherit the victorious life!

Questions

1. What are little steps you take to better your athletic skills?
2. What are some areas in your Christian life in which you must apply "due diligence?"

Further Reading

2 Peter 1:5-11; Deuteronomy 4:9, 6:7; Proverbs 4:23; Romans 12:11

Notes

27.

HEART OF A CHAMPION

*He who overcomes, I will grant to him to sit down with Me on
My throne, as I also overcame and sat down with
My Father on His throne.*
Revelation 3:21

The heart of a champion…Many talk about it; coaches seek to instill it in their players; players dream of being victorious. But what does the heart of a true champion look like?

Back in 2007, I, along with the rest of the world, watched one of the best tournament finals matches in the history of professional tennis. In this match, Roger Federer overcame a tremendous effort by Rafael Nadal to win his fifth Wimbledon championship. As the match progressed, the crowd was enthralled by the efforts of both athletes as they battled through adversity and staged comeback efforts to force the fifth set.

In the fifth set, Federer dug deep to find the will to win—that deep-seated determination to finish the task at hand. The final point, his tears of joy and the "coronation" of a new king of tennis were memorable. As I watched, I was reminded of a statement made by NBA Coach Rudy Tomjanovich after his team repeated as NBA Champions in 1995, "Don't ever underestimate the heart of a champion!"[21]

The night that Christ was betrayed, He spent time with His disciples. Before Jesus went to the Garden of Gethsemane that night, the last words He spoke to the disciples (as recorded by John) were, "These things I have spoken to you, so that in Me you may have peace. In the world you have tribulation, but take courage; I have overcome the world." (John 16:33).

Christ was the perfect example of a person with the heart of a champion. He completed the task at hand. He was obedient to the end. He endured the agony of the cross, the shame of public crucifixion, and the burden of sin placed on Him. He conquered death and overcame its grip to reclaim His throne next to His Father. Though He had the power of the universe in His hands, He remained humble and submitted to the will of His Father. And He emerged victorious!

In His message to the seven churches in Revelation, Christ gave a challenge. It was simple: "If you overcome, I will be there with you at the victor's stand!" As Christians, we are to develop the heart of a champion. We are to overcome the world and all its vices through the power of the Holy Spirit, which dwells within us. We are to complete the task God has given us to complete and fix our eyes on Him who endured His race to the end.

Questions

1. What does it take to develop the heart of a champion in your sport?
2. What does it take to develop the heart of a champion in the Christian life?

Further Reading

1 Corinthians 16:13-14; Hebrews 3:6

Notes

28.

STAND FIRM

Therefore, take up the full armor of God, so that you will be able to resist in the evil day, and having done everything, to stand firm. Stand firm therefore, HAVING GIRDED YOUR LOINS WITH TRUTH, and HAVING PUT ON THE BREASTPLATE OF RIGHTEOUSNESS, and having shod YOUR FEET WITH THE PREPARATION OF THE GOSPEL OF PEACE.
Ephesians 6:13-15 (emphasis in Bible version)

My younger brother was a decorated athlete as a high school and small college football player. One of my favorite memories was actually a game that did not go in his favor. That Friday night was a classic match-up between the top two teams in their conference...a matchup repeated countless times in towns small and large across this country every year. Both teams were highly rated for their dominant defense and offensive efficiency. Both teams entered the battle-field with spotless conference records. Both schools brought bus-loads of fans to the game, and the atmosphere was thick with pressure.

As in any classic battle, the match was well-played on both sides. That Friday night battle came down to the last stand. My brother's team was down by 4, with the ball on the one-yard line and four downs to get into the end-zone. "Defense," was the cry from across the field, "Stand Firm!"

Three plays later, the ball had moved a foot, with one final play...one chance to get into the end-zone or make a final stop. Our team tried an off-tackle run with seconds left...and met a wall of defenders. The defense held and preserved a hard-fought victory, and the match became the talk of every local restaurant the next morning.

STAND FIRM.

Those of us who have stood firm, stuck to the game-plan, and dug deep for that final, monumental, defensive effort can understand these words found in today's scripture.

We are involved in a spiritual war – we are the participants, and daily face challenges and tests designed to increase our faith. But there is also an enemy, lurking behind the scenes, whose intent is to challenge the mercy-seat of God. His intent is not to win a "game." His intent is to take your soul. Sometimes we may feel ill-equipped for the battle, but God has given us all that we need to stand firm against the enemy.

Through scripture, God tells us time and again to play strong defense. How?

We do so by putting on our armor: living a lifestyle of truth, obeying His commands, putting our full confidence in the Gospel, sitting deeply in faith, being equipped with God's word and undergirded with prayer. God developed a game-plan for us to follow. He Himself has already achieved the victory – but each of us must take a stand in the battle for our lives.

Questions

1. "Defense wins championships" is a generic axiom generally attributed to College Football legend Paul "Bear" Bryant. Why is a strong defense vital to being successful in most head to head sports?
2. Read Ephesians 6;13-18. Identify the different pieces of the armor of God and answer this question: What does each piece of armor look like in your life on a daily basis?

Further Reading

1 Corinthians 16:13; 2 Thessalonians 2:14-16

Notes

29.

DEDICATION

Suffer hardship with me, as a good soldier of Christ Jesus. No soldier in active service entangles himself in the affairs of everyday life, so that he may please the one who enlisted him as a soldier.
2 Timothy 2:3-4

Years ago, when I ran track in college, I had the privilege of doing workouts with several elite athletes who also trained at a particular facility in California. One of the athletes in my workout group was a promising college freshman named Mark Crear. Three years later, I watched his career take off after he finished third in the 110M High Hurdles at the NCAA Division 1 Track and Field Championships in 1990.

Over the span of the next 14 years, Crear emerged as one of the top 110M hurdlers in the world. As an Olympian with 2 Olympic medals, he held the #1 or #2 ranking in the world several times during that span. Crear endured many hardships throughout his career; he is often remembered for taking the silver medal in the 1996 Olympics with a cast on his broken arm.

Years later, I connected with Crear again when he came to the Midwest area to speak for a winter youth rally and local FCA event I had arranged. One day after speaking to my FCA huddle, he informed me he was going to do a workout. I showed him the indoor hallway where the team I was coaching ran in the winter months and let him get dressed in the locker room while I prepared for our high school team workout. I didn't see him for about 30 minutes and went to check on him…only to find him outside in a cold driving rain with the temperature hovering around 38 degrees.

When I asked him why he was out in the cold working out, he commented, 'Well, if you are going to run at the world class level, you realize the guy just behind you is outside working to catch you, and the guy ahead of you is outside somewhere working out because he knows you are working hard to catch him." That day I learned just how much Crear dedicated himself to the excellence necessary to achieve world-class status, the same dedication that defined this Christian athlete and set him apart from many others.

In his final letter to Timothy, Paul encourages his protégé to dedicate himself to his calling to serve God. Paul says, "No soldier in active service entangles himself in the affairs of everyday life" (2 Timothy 2:4). Soldiers live a life truly set apart for service. I remember living on the naval base as a child and recall vividly the life of preparedness my father lived on a daily basis. Daily, we see men and women dutifully serving overseas – not complaining about their jobs, the conditions, the struggle they are in. If asked why they put themselves in harm's way, many would simply answer, "I am serving my country."

As athletes and coaches, we each understand a level of dedication. We have set apart a portion of our days and lives for our particular sport. We endure the pain of workouts, three-a-days, and conditioning for the glory of victory. Let's apply that same dedication to Christ. Whether we are suffering doing God's will or simply trying to live day to day, we should dedicate all that we are (our thoughts, words, and deeds) to the Lord. Let's commit ourselves to our faithful Creator.

Questions

1. What does dedication look like for an athlete on a daily basis?
2. How do you set yourself apart from the world in your daily life?

Further Reading

1 Chronicles 23:13; Psalm 37:5; Proverbs 16:3;
1 Peter 4:19

Notes

30.

He Must Increase

He who has the bride is the bridegroom; but the friend of the bridegroom, who stands and hears him, rejoices greatly because of the bridegroom's voice. So this joy of mine has been made full. He must increase, but I must decrease.
John 3:29:30

John the Baptist was the man! He was the voice of God - the herald prophesied by Isaiah – "A voice of one crying in the wilderness" (John 1:23). He was the great baptizer of the people, the one who drew crowds everywhere he went. Yet he knew a time would come when his "star" status would diminish. John the Baptist proclaimed to be the herald of the Messiah...yet many assumed he himself was that man. However, he knew his role, and when Christ presented Himself for baptism, he graciously and humbly did so - then proclaimed to his followers, "Behold, the Lamb of God!" (John 1:29).

Can you imagine being there during this time of transition? I imagine it this way: John's disciples come to him saying, "John, that guy you yourself baptized, the crowds are going to him!" John must have smiled knowingly, maybe put a hand on his disciples' shoulders, and gently said, "I am not the man you seek. That man, Jesus, He is THE MAN. He is the Bride-groom, and I am his Best-Man...and I am glad for him. His time is come, and mine must fade." I can imagine the confidence in his voice as he points his disciples to Jesus.

Fast-forward to the 2008-09 NCAA Basketball season. Tyler Hansbrough, the reigning NCAA player of the year, had to make a choice for the sake of his team. In order to help his team attain their goal of a national championship, he was asked to take a "back seat" to teammate Ty Lawson. His scoring average fell, and he graciously passed the mantle of leadership to Lawson.

During one post-game interview in the post-season playoffs, he said, "I'm going to try to do whatever my team needs me to do to win."[22] This is a young man who knew his role and accepted the change in his role for the sake of the team. The result? Hansbrough, Lawson, and friends were crowned the 2009 National Champions.

If we are prone to envy, we will struggle with jealousy when a teammate is praised for a great performance. However, if we know our purpose and are fulfilling our role, how much easier it is to celebrate with them! If you know your purpose from God and your role in life, everything becomes a celebration of *Him*.

John knew this secret of life. Tyler Hansbrough understood this secret was a key to his team's success. Maybe we can learn from them how we as well can be good teammates and celebrate what others are doing...and what GOD is doing through them!

Questions

1. How do you handle seeing a teammate with more ability or gifts than you? How do you handle when a teammate receives praise and you do not?

2. In our personal walk, what steps can we take to overcome jealous tendencies?

Further Reading

1 Samuel 20; John 1:6-9, 19-28; John 3:22-30

Notes

31.

FOUGHT THE GOOD FIGHT

I have fought the good fight, I have finished the race,
I have kept the faith.
2 Timothy 4:7

Since the early 2000's, we clearly see the parity that exists at the highest level of college basketball during March Madness. It's always exciting to watch the thrilling overtime victories and the games that have been decided by three points or less. Teams are matched up toe-to-toe, scraped, hustled and competed to extend their seasons for one more game. At the end of every game, one team leaves the court celebrating while the other walks away empty-handed, perhaps stunned, that the game got away in the final ticks of the clock.

What strikes me the most almost every year is the number of players who are able to walk off the floor, look each other in the eye and say, "I left my all in the arena today." No, those words don't offer much consolation after a stunning loss, but they do mean quite a bit in the long run.

As a coach myself, I just think, "What more could a coach ask for?" Whether their team is outdone by talent or is evenly matched, every coach desires that their athletes give their best effort. Coaches understand that on any given day, if the ball bounces right and the whistles favor us, our teams have a chance to do something wonderful, *if* the effort is there.

Scripture offers us a glimpse at a very zealous person: the Apostle Paul. As a Pharisee, he zealously sought to root out the fledgling Christian church. Then, after he encountered Jesus on the road to Damascus, he was launched into a purpose-driven, Christian life. Paul counted it a privilege to suffer along with Christ, knowing that he suffered for the right reasons. Many of his epistles were written from a jail cell as he exhorted others to continue to grow in the faith and be transformed by the gospel. As his life drew to a close, he faced death with confidence and the assurance that he had poured out his life for Christ.

Many athletes competing in each year's tournament are zealous about a cause. They truly give their all for the game of basketball. Regardless of class, rank, school size or conference, they come to play. They come with a true sense of purpose because they were given a direction. Their coaches gave them a philosophy, which they bought into, and then gave them a game-plan to follow. They play with passion because they can go forth with confidence in their plan.

As Christians, we can do the same. We have a God who seeks to coach us and build a relationship of love and loyalty with us. He has given us a glimpse into His master plan and given us a game plan in His Word. As members of His team, we have to buy into His plan. We have to take risks for His sake because we trust that He will keep His promises. When we begin to do so, perhaps we will, as well, turn the world upside down just as Paul and the early Christians did.

Today, let's pour out our lives so we can echo Paul's words at the end of our journey. May we fight the good fight and finish the race.

Questions

1. In your experience, what gives you the confidence you need in order to finish your games well?
2. What scriptures give you confidence in God's plan for your life?

Further Reading

Jeremiah 29:11; Matthew 10; 2 Timothy 4:6-8

Notes

SOURCES

All Scriptures from
New American Standard Bible (NASB). The Lockman
Foundation, 1995.

Chapter 1: How's Your Foundation
1-@TullianT. "We often rest our Christianity on the
crumbling foundation of our imperfect devotion to
Jesus rather than on his perfect devotion to us."
Twitter, 17 May 2012, 8:09am, https://twitter.com/
TullianT/status/203140064178475009.

Chapter 4: God Qualifies the Called
2-"God Can Use Us All." *Bible.org,* 20 July 2009,
https://bible.org/illustration/god-can-use-us-all.

Chapter 5: Dream Big
3-Stein, Jean. "William Faulkner, The Art of Fiction No.
12." *The Paris Review,* iss. 12, spring 1956,
https://www.theparisreview.org/interviews/4954/will
iam-faulkner-the-art-of-fiction-no-12-william-faulkner.

Chapter 8: Win-Win Situation
4-Chapman, Michael W. "U.S. Gold Medalist Gabby
Douglas: 'I Give All the Glory to God.'" *CNS
News.com,* 3 August 2012, https://www.cnsnews
.com/news/article/us-gold-medalist-gabby-douglas-i-
give-all-glory-god.

Chapter 9: Mastering the Ordinary

5-Chambers, Oswald. "October 21: Direction by Impulse." *My Utmost for His Highest*. Classic ed., Barbour Books, 1999.

Chapter 11: Desire

6-"Bill Shoemaker Quotes." BrainyQuote.com. Xplore Inc, 2018. 11 May 2018. https://www.brainyquote.com/quotes/bill_shoemaker_158941

7-"Lexicon :: Strong's H8378 - ta'avah." *Blue Letter Bible*, 2018, https://www.blueletterbible.org/lang/lexicon/lexicon.cfm?Strongs=H8378&t=NASB.

8-"Lexicon :: Strong's H7592 - sha'al." *Blue Letter Bible*, 2018, https://www.blueletterbible.org/lang/lexicon/lexicon.cfm?Strongs=H7592&t=NASB

Chapter 12: Spreading the Salt

9-Meyer, Clay. "Mastering the Game." *Sharing the Victory: Faith and Sport*, June/July 2010, https://archives.fca.org/vsItemDisplay.lsp?method=display&objectid=BF767F2B-C29A-EE7A-E3430FE24128DA07

Chapter 14: Order My Steps: The Right Direction

10-Hedrick, Chad. "Being a Christian is More Than Saying You're a Christian." *Haven Today*, 18 February 2010, http://www.haventoday.org/series/being-a-christian-is-more-than-saying-youre-a-christian/.

Chapter 16: Defining Moments

11-Moran, Dan. "Career & Life 2.0: Your Defining Moment: Here's Your Sign…" *Times Union*, 8 February 2015, https://blog.timesunion.com/careers/career-life-2-0- your-defining-moment-heres-your-sign/3099/.

Chapter 18: Home Crowd: Cloud of Witnesses

12-Eaton, Ashton. "Ashton Eaton After His 9039 Decathlon World Record With Trey Hardee and Gray Horn." *YouTube,* uploaded by letsrundotcom, 23 June 2012, https://www.youtube.com/watch?v=-0fXozWIL3U.

Chapter 20: An Expensive Mistake

13-"Sven Kramer mistake hands 10,000m gold to Korea's Lee." *BBC Sport,* 23 February 2010, http://news.bbc.co.uk/sport2/hi/olympic_games/vancouver_2010/speed_skating/8533237.stm.

Chapter 22: Words of Grace

14-Ginott, Haim G. *Teacher and Child: A Book for Parents and Teachers.* Scribner Paper, 1993.

Chapter 23: Two are Better Than One

15-Hinton, Ed. "Gordon, Johnson save their best for last at Talladega." *LATimes,* 8 October 2007, http://articles.latimes.com/2007/oct/08/sports/sp-nascar8.

Chapter 26: Diligence

16-Wooden, John. *Wooden on Leadership.* 1st ed., McGraw Hill, 2005.

17-"Diligence." *The Free Dictionary by Farlex,* 2003-2018, https://www.thefreedictionary.com/diligence.

18-"Diligence." *English Oxford Living Dictionaries,* 2018, https://en.oxforddictionaries.com/definition/diligence.

19-"Lexicon :: Strong's H8104 - shamar." *Blue Letter Bible,* 2018, https://www.blueletterbible.org/lang/lexicon/lexicon.cfm?t=kjv&strongs=h8104.

20-"Spoude." *Bible Study Tools,* 2018 https://www.biblestudytools.com/lexicons/greek/kjv/spoude.html.

Chapter 27: Heart of a Champion

21-Tomjanovich, Rudy. "Don't ever underestimate the heart of a champion." *YouTube,* uploaded by Karol K, 7 May 2007, https://www.youtube.com/watch?v=5-1jgNhopNo.

Chapter 30: He Must Increase

22-"Tar Heels address Griffin, OU, lack of cookies." *Wral SPORTSfan,* 28 March 2009, https://www.wralsports fan.com/unc/story/4835200/.

ABOUT THE EDITOR

Faith Sayles is a dancer and a writer who seeks out beauty and stories to share with others. She graduated from Anderson University (IN) with a Bachelor of Arts in Dance Business and Writing. This is Faith's first time serving as the editor of a book and she hopes to continue working as an editor. Faith is passionate about using her gifts to worship God and help others see His beauty. She loves books, language, anime, and traveling.

To learn more about Faith, visit her website faithsayles.org.

ABOUT THE GRAPHIC DESIGNER

Alena Nead is a multi-talented creative constantly seeking to expand her portfolio. She grew up in southern Illinois and will obtain (2019) her Bachelor of Arts in Visual Communications Design and Dance Performance at Anderson University in Indiana. Alena is passionate about using her multiple art forms to glorify God and uplift others. She is an avid fan of books, white tigers, and anything and everything pink!

To find out more about Alena, follow Alena's Graphic Design at http://designbyalena.com or on Facebook at @graphicdesignbyalena.